The Autism-Friendly Guide to Periods

by the same author

The Independent Woman's Handbook for Super Safe Living on the Autistic Spectrum
ISBN 978 1 84905 399 0
eISBN 978 0 85700 765 0

of related interest

What's Happening to Ellie?
A book about puberty for girls and young women
with autism and related conditions
Kate E. Reynolds
Illustrated by Jonathon Powell
ISBN 978 1 84905 526 0
eISBN 978 0 85700 937 1
Part of the Sexuality and Safety with Tom and Ellie series

The Growing Up Guide for Girls
What Girls on the Autism Spectrum Need to Know!
Davida Hartman
Illustrated by Margaret Anne Suggs
ISBN 978 1 84905 574 1
eISBN 978 1 78450 038 2
Part of the Growing Up series

M is for Autism
The Students of Limpsfield Grange School and Vicky Martin
ISBN 978 1 84905 684 7
eISBN 978 1 78450 198 3

Camouflage
The Hidden Lives of Women with Autism
Sarah Bargiela
Illustrated by Sophie Standing
ISBN 978 1 78592 566 5
eISBN 978 1 78592 667 9

Girls Growing Up on the Autism Spectrum
What Parents and Professionals Should Know
About the Pre-Teen and Teenage Years
Shana Nichols with Gina Marie Moravcik
and Samara Pulver Tetenbaum
ISBN 978 1 84310 855 9
eISBN 978 1 84642 885 2

The Autism-Friendly Guide to Periods

Robyn Steward

Jessica Kingsley *Publishers*
London and Philadelphia

First published in 2019
by Jessica Kingsley Publishers
73 Collier Street
London N1 9BE, UK
and
400 Market Street, Suite 400
Philadelphia, PA 19106, USA

www.jkp.com

Library of Congress Cataloging in Publication Data
A CIP catalog record for this book is available from the Library of Congress

British Library Cataloguing in Publication Data
A CIP catalogue record for this book is available from the British Library

ISBN 978 1 78592 324 1
eISBN 978 1 78450 637 7

Printed and bound in China

Contents

The frame

A note from the author

Hello, I'm Robyn and I wrote this book.

I know that periods might seem a bit grown up, complicated and worrying (whether you are a kid or a parent or guardian). As with many things in life it can take some time to get used to new things, but I have tried to make the information in this book less overwhelming.

I have made a frame that you can cut out on the previous page. The frame page has six boxes marked out. Cut three sides of each box to create six flaps (or windows).

On some pages, I have designed the page to have a grid of six squares. Place the template over a page and then you can use the flaps (windows) to hide or view the contents of each square.

You can practise using the frame with the two photographs of me at the bottom of this page.

Part 1

The Basics

What Are Periods?

1.1 What a period is and what it isn't

Before I explain what a period is, it helps to know that your body produces some things that are supposed to come out of it. For example, the saliva (spit) in your mouth is made to keep your mouth clean and help you swallow. When you brush your teeth you spit out some saliva with the toothpaste and your body makes more saliva. By spitting out the saliva you are not harmed in any way and have not lost something which cannot be replaced. The same is true of poo. Your body gets rid of the waste from things you eat by producing poo (the scientific name for this is 'faeces'). Every human has a mouth where saliva is produced and a bottom where poo comes out.

Some people have a body part inside them called a womb (also called a uterus). Wombs make a lining that comes out of the body regularly as a way of cleaning the womb. When the womb lining and blood come out of a hole between the legs called a vagina, this is known as a period.

Having a period does not need to be scary. (There are lots of things to help it to feel less scary.)

A period does not stop you from doing anything.

Note: These answers are deliberately simple. I am starting slowly, but there is a lot more detail in the rest of the book.

What is a period?	What isn't a period?
Periods happen every four to six weeks.	A period is not an illness.
A period is one way in which most bodies that have a womb keep healthy.	A period does not mean you are injured or hurt.
Periods happen to almost half of all humans in the world at some point in their lives.	A period does not mean a person is a fully grown woman.

1.2 Who has periods?

Below are some examples of real people who have periods. Your teachers, mum and friends' mums will all have periods or know someone who does. Periods are a normal part of life. I have put adults on this page because I want you to know that you can ask for help from adults. They started having periods between the age of 8 and 16 and they got through it, so you will too!

Carley – mum

Emma – teacher

Robyn – author

Ella – social worker

Sarah – actress

Kathryn – sales assistant

1.3 Why some people have periods and some people don't

People who have periods have a womb (which is sometimes called a uterus), ovaries, fallopian tubes and a vagina. Together these are sometimes called the female reproductive system.

The vagina is a tube with an opening to the outside of the body between the legs. (In this area most people who have periods also have a hole for pee called the urethra, and one for poo called the anus.) In this book you will learn more about the vagina, uterus, fallopian tubes and ovaries.

Normally the area between the legs is called the private parts or genitals. They are the parts of our body covered by underwear. It is very important to keep these parts of your body private. Have a look at the NSPCC PANTS campaign to find out more about this.

Some people with a vagina, uterus, fallopian tubes and ovaries (or some of these parts) might not have periods because of a health condition or a medical treatment, or because they are older and their periods have stopped.

People with a male reproductive system do not have periods.

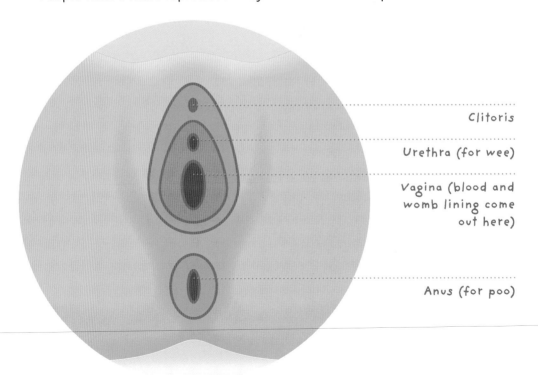

Clitoris

Urethra (for wee)

Vagina (blood and womb lining come out here)

Anus (for poo)

1.4 Why people who don't have periods still need to know about them

Some people who don't have periods are shown below. They need to understand how different people may experience periods so they can be supportive. It is important to talk about them to avoid any misunderstandings and reduce embarrassment.

Mark – dad

David – uncle

Sam – friend

Ken – friend/teacher

Rick – bandmate

Tim – teacher/dad

1.5 What are the internal parts of the body involved in periods?

What do the inside parts of the body that make periods happen look like?

Some parts of the body can't be seen from the outside. On the next page you can see a drawing of the parts of the body that make periods happen.

1. Ovaries

The ovaries are where eggs grow. These eggs are very tiny.

They are not like chicken eggs!

2. Fallopian tubes

The fallopian tubes are how the eggs get to the womb. They are not connected directly to the ovaries, but have tentacle-like strands that wave the eggs down the tube towards the womb.

3. Womb

The womb is hollow and muscular. It builds up a lining which is shed as a period.

If an egg is fertilised it implants in the wall of the womb.

4. Ligaments

The ligaments hold the uterus and ovaries in place.

5. Vagina

The vagina is a sloped tube of muscle that connects the womb to the outside of the body.

The womb lining leaves the body through the vagina.

The diagram on the next page shows how these parts all fit together.

These parts are known as the reproductive system. I am not going into detail about that here because you will learn about it in other places (and you may not want to know about it now).

But it is important to know that this is the reason some people have periods. The uterus needs to keep its lining fresh. A period is the old lining of the uterus coming away so it can be replaced by a fresh one. Chemicals in your blood make your muscles around your uterus tense up and then relax over and over to make the old lining come out. (The tensing and relaxing of your muscles is called a cramp.) Periods last between two and seven days because it takes this long for the old lining to leave the body.

How big are these parts of the body?

This diagram is made from household objects to make it easier to understand the size of the body parts I've been talking about.

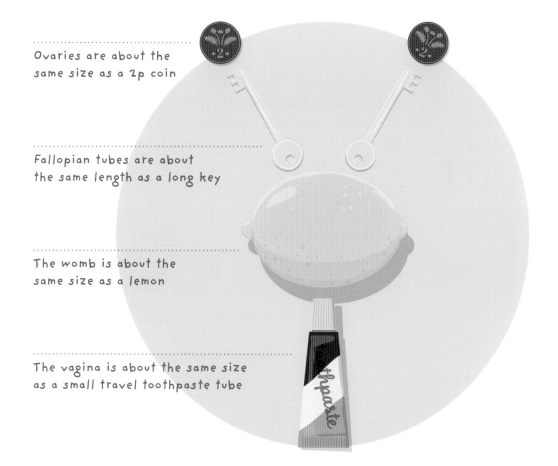

Ovaries are about the same size as a 2p coin

Fallopian tubes are about the same length as a long key

The womb is about the same size as a lemon

The vagina is about the same size as a small travel toothpaste tube

1.6 Blood! Am I hurt?

You may only ever have seen blood when you have been hurt. For example, you may have fallen over in the playground, or cut your finger.

But blood can come out of the body when a person is not hurt, for example when a person gives blood (they go to a blood bank and a nurse takes some of their blood to be given to people who need it, such as when they have an operation).

For people who have periods, the blood is actually keeping them healthy because it means the old uterus lining is coming out so their body can make a fresh one. A period is the first part of something called a menstrual cycle.

The amount of blood that comes out of the body during a period is 40–120 ml. See Section 3.1 to work out how much this is.

1.7 The menstrual cycle

What's a 'cycle'?

A cycle is a pattern of things happening. For example, at night-time the sky *mostly* looks black and sometimes you can see the moon and stars. After night-time the sun rises and it is daytime. In the daytime the sky is usually blue. *Sometimes* there are clouds that are white or grey. The sun being visible and not visible and the moon being visible and not visible is a cycle.

So what's a 'menstrual cycle'?

A menstrual cycle is the pattern of things a person's body does to menstruate (this is the scientific word for having a period). Menstrual cycles can take between three and six weeks.

On the next pages you can find out what happens each week if a person has a four-week menstrual cycle. You may have some, none or all of the symptoms described. It's just important to know they could happen.

Remember that some people's menstrual cycles can be shorter or longer than four weeks and still be normal.

1.8 What happens during a menstrual cycle?

Once you start to have menstrual cycles, the cycle will repeat around every four weeks, meaning that you will always be experiencing a part of the cycle (although you only bleed in week 1). The table below shows you what happens each week.

Week 1

The uterus lining and some blood come out of the vagina over about a week. This is called a period.

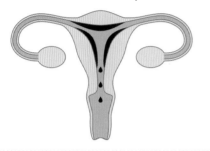

Emotional symptoms

Some people:

- feel tired
- lack confidence
- have PMS/PMT symptoms

Or they might feel:

- curious
- positive
- tolerant
- more sociable.

Physical symptoms

Some people have:

- achy muscles
- stomach ache
- back ache
- bloating
- changes in appetite.

Week 2

The uterus starts to build up a new lining.

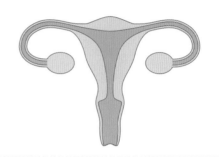

Emotional symptoms

People sometimes feel:

- giggly
- confident
- impulsive
- more attractive.

Physical symptoms

People sometimes have a:

- heightened sense of smell
- headache
- stomach ache.

Some people feel less sensitive to pain.

Not everyone will experience all of the emotional and physical symptoms described below, and the PMS/PMT (premenstrual syndrome/premenstrual tension) symptoms experienced by some people often get better after week 1, but everyone's bodies will do the things shown in the pictures.

Week 3

An egg is released from one of the ovaries and moves down the fallopian tube to the uterus.

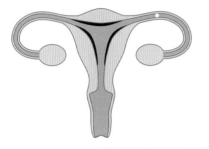

Emotional symptoms
People sometimes feel:

- sad
- sleepy
- quiet
- less sociable.

They might find it hard to think. PMS/PMT may start.

Physical symptoms
Some people have food cravings.

Week 4

The lining of the uterus continues to grow.

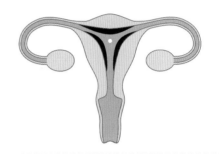

Emotional symptoms
Some people feel:

- angry
- irritated
- gloomy
- sensitive
- anxious
- tired.

Physical symptoms
Some people have:

- diarrhoea or constipation
- muscle ache
- breast sensitivity
- bloating
- food cravings.

Period Supplies

2.1 How do you stop the blood and uterus lining going everywhere?

There are lots of options for collecting the blood from a period so it doesn't stain your clothes, bedding or furniture (though stains can be cleaned easily). These are known as menstruation supplies and can also be called:

- feminine hygiene products
- fem-care
- sanitary products
- menstrual products.

Some period supplies are used inside the body, some are used instead of underwear, and some are put inside underwear.

Using the frame, lift each of the flaps on the left to see a photo of a collection method and the opposite flap to read some information about it.

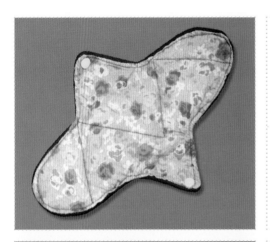

Menstrual cloth

These are made from a choice of different fabrics.

They are put inside underwear and changed a few times a day.

They can be washed in a washing machine.

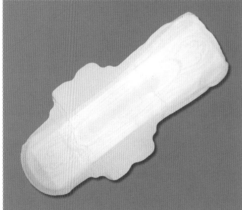

Pad

These are disposable.

They are made from fabric and have a sticky back which is used to hold it in place in your underwear.

They are changed every few hours and you throw them away when used.

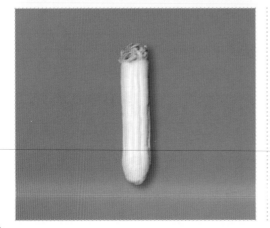

Tampon

These are inserted into your vagina.

They expand as blood and womb lining falls onto them.

They are taken out and thrown away every few hours.

Menstrual cup

These are folded and inserted into your vagina (they open out once inside your vagina).

The blood and womb lining falls into the cup which is then removed, emptied and replaced every 8–12 hours (depending on the brand of menstrual cup used).

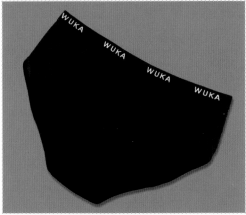

Period underwear

This is worn like normal underwear.

It has several layers of special fabric designed to catch and hold blood and womb lining.

It can be worn for a full day, depending on the brand and type, and how much blood you lose (your blood flow).

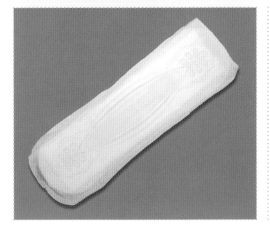

Panty liner

These are like pads but they are worn when people are now quite sure when their periods are going to start.

They can't be worn for a whole period as they are not very absorbent.

2.2 Tampons

What is a tampon?

Tampons are soft and shaped a little like a tablet/pill. You put a tampon inside your vagina where it expands and absorbs fluids.

Because your vagina is made from muscle it will hold the tampon in place, but it stays soft so it is also easy to take the tampon out.

In culture

Lots of people use tampons; however, some cultures and religions feel that using a tampon is the same as losing your virginity (although without sex) and forbid people to use them before marriage.

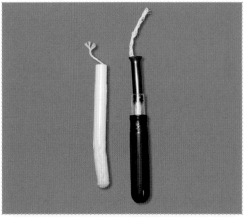

Applicator tampons

An applicator is made from two small tubes of cardboard or plastic with the tampon inside. You insert it into your vagina and gently push one of the tubes to insert the tampon. You then take out the applicator and throw it away.

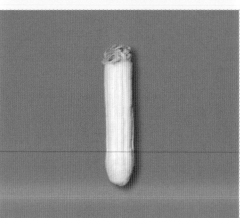

Non-applicator tampons

Tampons without an applicator are inserted into your vagina using your fingers.

You are more likely to get blood on your fingers when you insert or take out a non-applicator tampon than if you use an applicator tampon.

How much blood can a tampon hold?

Light/lite: less than 6 ml

Regular: 6–9 ml

Super: 9–12 ml

Super plus: 12–15 ml

Ultra: 15–18 ml

Toxic shock syndrome (TSS)

This is an illness associated with tampon use. It is more likely to happen if you leave a tampon inside your vagina for too long. See the tampon packet to find out how long you can use them.

TSS is rare, but you should read about the symptoms of TSS in Section 3.9.

How often should tampons be changed?

Tampons need to be changed regularly; see the manufacturer's guidance for more information.

Helpful info

Very occasionally a tampon gets beyond reach. If this happens you can try squatting, which will make your vagina shorter, and also pushing with your vagina muscles. If this doesn't work you should go to a doctor so they can remove it.

Pros

You can swim with a tampon in.

Tampons can be found in many shops.

Tampons are small and discreet.

Cons

Can cause TSS.

Can be difficult to insert at first.

It is not advisable to wear a tampon overnight, but check the information in the box of the tampons you want to use, or on the manufacturer's website, and follow their advice.

2.3 Pads

What is a pad?
Pads are made from layers of fabric and plastic.

Perfume
Some pads have a scent added, though it is possible to get unscented ones.

Unscented pads can sometimes smell a little. However, do not worry about this – other people will not be able to smell it even if they sit close to you.

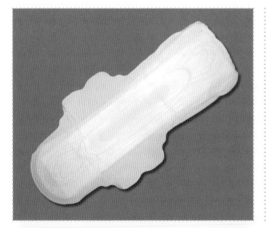

Wings
Some pads have wings. These are sticky flaps which you stick around your underwear to hold the pad in place.

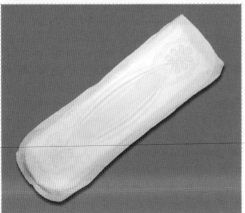

No wings
Some pads do not have wings (the packets usually say if they have wings or not).
The back of the pad is sticky and is pressed onto your underwear.

How often should pads be changed?

Some pads can be worn for up to ten hours, but most will last around three to four hours.

You should change it whenever it feels uncomfortable.

How to use

Stick the pad onto your underwear when you have a period.

Change the pad every few hours (see packet for instructions). You will get used to what a pad looks like when it is full.

Throw away when used.

Where to get them

Pads are available in shops like newsagents, pharmacies/drugstores and supermarkets.

Helpful info

Pads are sometimes known as sanitary pads, sanitary napkins, menstrual pads or sanitary towels.

Pros

Easy to buy from supermarkets, newsagents and pharmacies/drugstores.

There is no evidence that they can cause TSS.

Easy to put on and use.

Can be worn when you are not on your period, such as when you think your period may start.

Cons

Can feel a bit wet when full.

Can get smelly.

Often not biodegradable.

2.4 Menstrual cloths/pads

What is a menstrual cloth?

Menstrual cloths can be handmade or bought, e.g. from Etsy, eBay, Lunapads or Feminine Wear. They have three layers:

- top (goes against your skin)
- middle/core (holds the fluids)
- backing (goes next to your underwear).

In culture

Many people in developing countries use cloth menstrual pads as they do not have access to pads or tampons.

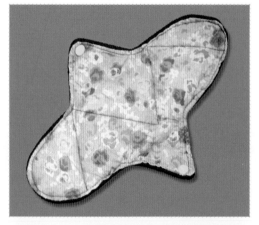

How to use

Use the poppers (snaps) to secure the pad around your underwear.

Use a wet bag (a waterproof bag with two zippable compartments) to store your clean and used pads separately.

Machine wash them.

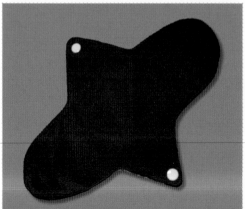

Wicking

The top layer of the pads are made from wicking, a fabric that sucks up liquid to the layer behind it so that the pad doesn't leak and you feel drier and more comfortable.

How often should menstrual cloths be changed?

This varies according to their construction and your flow, but could be from every two to eight hours.

Custom

You can make your own pads to any length you want. Typical lengths are:

- panty liners: 15cm/6″
- light/medium flow: 20cm/8″
- heavy flow/night: 25cm/10″.

For instructions for making your own pads, visit www.autismfriendlyperiods.com/makeclothpads.

Helpful info

Menstrual cloths can be made with lots of different fabric textures, colours and patterns, which can provide more stimulation for those who need it and less stimulation for those who don't.

Pros

Customisable for sensory needs.

Easy to buy online.

Different patterns available.

Can be worn when not on a period.

Very comfortable.

Washed at home so you can control the smell of the clean pads.

Cons

Not easy to buy in shops.

You have to be organised to bring clean pads and the wet bag.

You need to wash them yourself.

You need to be able to organise yourself to wash the pads.

You need to have enough of them to get through your period.

2.5 Menstrual cups

What is a menstrual cup?

Menstrual cups are small soft cups which you fold and insert into your vagina where they open to catch the blood.

Then they can be removed, emptied into the toilet, rinsed and reinserted into the vagina.

They are usually made from medical grade silicone.

In culture

As with tampons, some cultures and religions do not allow the use of menstrual cups.

Medical grade silicone

Medical grade silicone is silicone that has been approved for use in medical devices.

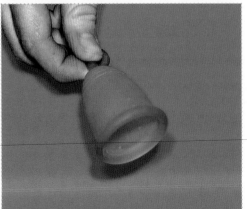

TPE

TPE (thermoplastic elastomer) is a type of plastic used for making baby bottle teats. It is softer than medical grade silicone so may be better for someone just starting to use a cup.

TSS

No link to TSS but you should sterilise your menstrual cup at the end and start of each cycle.

Folds

There are several kinds of folds you can use. Three common folds are:

- 7 fold
- punch fold
- C fold.

To see the different folds, visit www.autismfriendlyperiods.com/cupfolds.

How often should menstrual cups be emptied?

The cup should be emptied every 8–12 hours. (If you're in a public/school toilet and don't want to wash your cup in front of other people, just empty it in the toilet and put it back inside your vagina.)

Helpful info

It can take several cycles for some people to learn to use menstrual cups.

Pros

You only need one menstrual cup, which will last for up to ten years (depending on the type).

You are less likely to feel damp, which sometimes happens with pads.

You don't feel it inside you.

You can swim with it in.

Cons

Can be hard to find in high street shops.

Means putting your fingers inside your vagina (which some people find difficult, though they can soon get used to it).

Can be difficult to use to begin with.

2.6 Period underwear

What is period underwear?
Period underwear is underwear designed to catch menstrual blood and fluids, and absorb them.

Swimming
You can get swimming bottoms (bikini bottoms) and swimsuits which can be worn during a period.

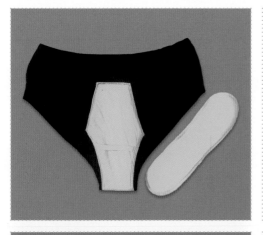

Inserts
Some period underwear has fabric loops which inserts can be placed into.

The inserts work like cloth menstrual pads.

No insert
This kind of period underwear can be worn as you would normal underwear.

It has several layers of fabric (but can still be very comfortable to wear).

It comes in lots of different styles such as shorts as well as feminine designs.

How often should period underwear be changed?

Period underwear should be changed every 4–14 hours, depending on the design and your flow.

Helpful info

Lots of different styles are available so you can get ones which are comfortable for you.

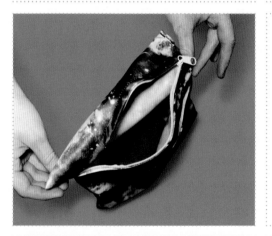

Storing period underwear

You can store period underwear with your non-period underwear.

You can carry spare and used inserts in a wet bag (a waterproof bag with two zippable compartments).

Pros

You can wear them as normal underwear when not on a period.

You can buy heavy flow underwear so that you only need to change once a day.

They can be washed so you don't have to keep buying disposable menstrual products.

Cons

Can be expensive initially.

Not easy to buy on the high street (though available online).

Inserts can be tricky to use at first.

2.7 Where to keep sanitary products

It's important that you keep some period supplies easily accessible at all times. If you are at home they can stay in the bathroom or your bedroom, but if you go out you must carry them with you, as sometimes periods can start unexpectedly. Below are some pictures of places you could keep your products. Tick the ones you will use, and maybe add your own ideas.

Form/home room teacher's desk

Locker

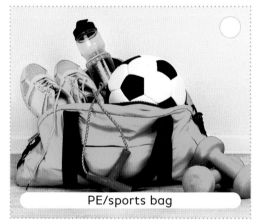
PE/sports bag

School bag

Musical instrument case

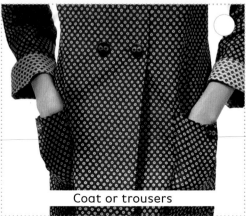
Coat or trousers

2.8 Where to dispose of used sanitary products

Disposable sanitary products (tampons and pads) need to be disposed of properly. In most bathrooms or toilet cubicles there will be a bin for sanitary products at the side of the toilet.

Below are some examples of the kinds of bins which you might see.

Foot-operated bins

These have a pedal at the bottom (close to the floor).

Press the pedal with your foot and the top of the bin will open.

Keep your foot on the pedal while you put your used tampon/pad in the bin, then release the pedal.

Hand-operated bins

Pull up on the handle (if this doesn't work try lifting the handle up and moving your hand back or forward) or push the lid.

Sensory-operated bins

Put your hand just above the sensor (usually a small black piece of plastic on the top of the bin). Then take your hand away and the lid should open by itself.

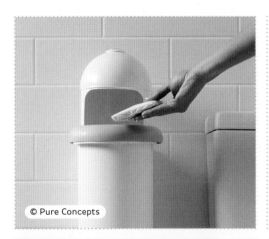

© Pure Concepts

Shapes of bins

- Wall mounted
- Thin box
- Bigger box
- Slot
- Sanipod
- Bathroom bin (at home or a friend's house)

In some schools, large office blocks and other commercial places there might be no bin in the cubicle but a unit like the one pictured on the left, which has paper towels above and a bin below.

What if there's no bin?

If you find there is no bin, you can either take your pad/tampon wrapped in toilet paper to a bin outside the bathroom or carry a plastic bag with you. You can then put the pad or tampon in the plastic bag and dispose of it when you get home (or to a bathroom with a bin).

Common Period Worries

3.1 How much blood will there be?

The amount of blood lost in each period is around 40–120 ml.

To understand how much this is, measure out 120 ml of water (about 24 teaspoons) into a jug (remember, this amount of menstrual blood and lining would come out of your vagina over around a week, and not in one day). If you want you can add some food colouring to the water and try pouring it onto pads and tampons or into a menstrual cup to give you a better understanding of how much blood each item can hold.

The amount of blood you lose is also known as your blood flow, for example heavy blood flow = lots of blood.

3.2 What if blood leaks onto my clothes?

If your pad/tampon/cup is full or not quite in the right place then blood may run onto your clothes or bedding. Don't panic – this does not mean you have failed. It is something that happens to most people who have periods.

Tips:

- When you first start your periods you may want to try changing your pad or tampon, or emptying your cup, every couple of hours until you get an idea of what it feels like when it needs to be changed.
- If you get blood on your top or trousers you can tie a jumper around your shoulders or waist so it covers the stained area.
- Try to pack spare underwear in your bag.
- If blood leaks onto your bedding/clothing/furniture it can easily be cleaned up by putting salt over the blood and rubbing it in with a cold damp cloth (salt and cold water break up the blood cells and take out the stain), then just put your bedding in the wash.
- You can also use salt and cold water on your clothes to remove blood stains.
- If you are very worried about leaking and you are using a tampon or menstrual cup you could also wear a pad/panty liner or period underwear. If you are wearing a pad or menstrual cloth you could also wear period underwear.

3.3 Are periods dirty?

No. Some people think that periods are dirty, and get worried about germs. Germs or 'bacteria' are things which can cause illness and disease.

In the human body we have 'good' bacteria, which help to kill things that should not be in our body. Each part of the body (e.g. the stomach, the vagina) needs different amounts of bacteria. In each of these areas, the bacteria that live there are designed just for that area and are different in each person.

When these bacteria leave the area they are designed for it can lead to illness. It is important to change your pad or tampon regularly to avoid a build-up of bacteria being in contact with your skin. If you do not change your menstrual product regularly then bacteria can start growing on the menstrual product and this can be smelly and make you uncomfortable.

(Note that you can wear a menstrual cup for longer than tampons as the blood is not in contact with your skin, and just stays in the cup.)

It is important to wash your hands after changing your menstrual product because your hands and the things you touch with them (e.g. your mouth, nose, ears or eyes) have their own level of bacteria that is different to the level in your vagina.

If you wash your hands after using a sanitary bin there is no need to worry that you're going to get an illness, but if you do want to take an extra precaution, then wrap your hand in toilet paper before placing your pad/tampon in the bin. Most sanitary bins also contain a germicide, which can make the bin smell (it doesn't always smell bad but can emit an odour). This is to reduce the small risk of infections being passed on to someone else using the same sanitary bin.

Before putting your fingers inside your vagina wash them first so they are clean, and wash them again after you have inserted or taken out the menstrual product so that you don't leave blood on your fingers which can get sticky.

3.4 Are periods painful?

Some people experience pain when they have a period, and some people do not. Both experiences are normal. Also, the same person may find some periods more painful than others. The pain is not the same as being hurt when you have an accident (such as falling over). It does not mean there is anything wrong with you. The pain is caused by the muscles around your uterus squeezing your uterus really tightly to help the old lining out. Because the lining is being pushed out by the muscles squeezing it is called a cramp.

Some people also get back pain. This pain usually reduces and does not have to last the whole period. Some people only get a little pain on the first day, and some people don't get any pain at all.

What can help with period pain?

As with other kinds of pain (such as headaches), there are things you can do to reduce the pain. Here is a list of some things that a lot of people find helpful. Tick the ones that you think would help you.

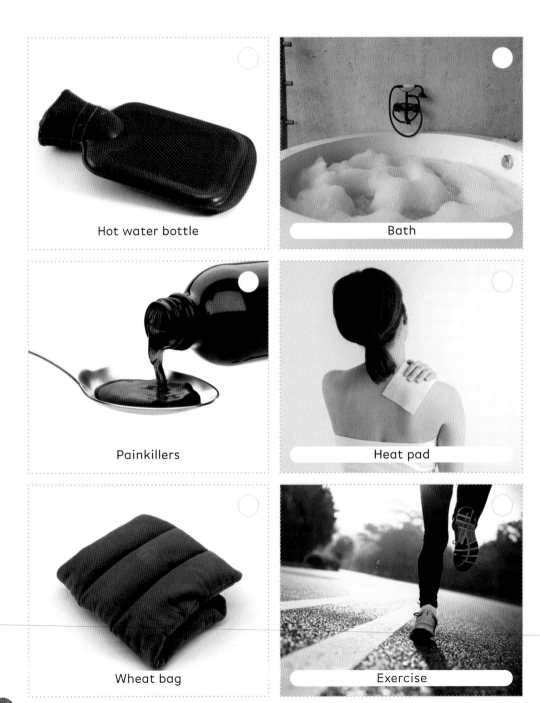

Hot water bottle

Bath

Painkillers

Heat pad

Wheat bag

Exercise

3.5 Do periods affect your mood?

Some people experience big emotions just before or during their period. This doesn't happen to everyone so it's OK if you don't. These big emotions can feel overwhelming and can change your behaviour. For example, when people are sad they often cry. The emotion is sad and the behaviour that is caused by being sad is crying. This is because hormones (chemicals released into your body as part of the menstrual cycle) can affect how you experience the world.

When emotions are difficult to cope with before or during a period this is called premenstrual syndrome (PMS) or premenstrual tension (PMT). PMS/PMT does not affect everybody, and it starts to go away when you start your period. Some people report being moody and argumentative just before their period, but then feel much calmer when they start their period.

It can be useful to think about the emotions you may have during PMS/PMT and what you can do about them, so that you are in control rather than your hormones. Below are some examples of emotions to help you get started. At the end of this list is a table you can fill out in the book, or you can draw your own.

Irritable

Being irritable means that you feel annoyed easily. When people are feeling like this they sometimes react to what would usually seem a small thing as if it were bigger. For example, for some people losing something is normally just annoying and they might think about it for a few minutes but when someone is irritable they might be thinking about it for an hour.

When people are irritable they might speak in a way that makes others feel bad (sometimes speaking quickly or implying that they think the other person is stupid).

Sad

When people feel sad it is often because they feel that they have missed out doing something, that they regret something that has happened (this could be something they have done or not done), or they miss someone or something a lot. Sometimes people feel sad because they see someone else is feeling sad.

People sometimes cry when they are sad.

Their behaviour can change in other ways, for example if they are usually chatty they may go very quiet, i.e. not talking very much.

Sometimes people feel sad for no reason at all (this is OK and will pass).

Anxious

Being anxious is when you think a lot about something that is going to happen (or might happen or is happening) and think about the bad outcomes. For example, if you were anxious about a test you would be thinking about how you might fail or get low grades, or what your friends might say or if you will be put into another group.

Sometimes people can go quiet when they are anxious because they are thinking about what it is that is making them anxious.

Sometimes people can become very talkative about what is making them anxious.

Sometimes people want to be told that everything is going to be OK.

Being anxious can also give you stomach ache and can make you want to go to the toilet a lot.

Angry

Being angry is sometimes called being in a bad temper or being cross.

It means that something or someone has made you feel bad, for example because you think they should have known something they didn't, they did something to upset or hurt you, or you didn't get to do something because they said you couldn't or stopped you from doing it.

Being angry can make a person want to shout and slam doors.

When someone is angry their behaviour can make others feel scared.

Overwhelmed

Feeling overwhelmed is when one or more of the ways your body and brain process information gets too much information.

This could be too many emotions (or too much of one or more emotion), too much information from one or more of your senses (e.g. smell), or too much to think about (such as when something goes wrong and you have to come up with a new plan for the day).

Meltdowns

A meltdown often happens when someone is overwhelmed.

It can look to others like a tantrum; however, if a child is having a tantrum and the adult gives in to their demands, the tantrum will stop. A meltdown will continue, because it is not a deliberate behaviour – it is happening because the world has become too much.

Shutdowns

Like meltdowns, shutdowns are not a choice.

Shutdowns are where someone withdraws from their environment.

This could be by getting under a table, pulling a hoody over their head, or not responding to their name (make sure there is no medical reason for them not responding – an epileptic seizure can look similar to a shutdown).

Again, shutdowns are often caused by being overwhelmed.

Irritable

Draw or write down something that irritates you.

Sad

Draw or write down something that makes you sad.

Anxious

Draw or write down something that makes you anxious.

Angry
Draw or write down something that makes you angry.

Overwhelmed
Draw or write down something that makes you feel overwhelmed.

Meltdowns and shutdowns
Draw or write down something that makes you have meltdowns or shutdowns.

You may want to try making a table like the one below to mark when you have these emotions within your menstrual cycle so you can see when they happen (and if there is a pattern). You don't have to have them every day of a week to put a mark in that week's box. You can also add your own emotions.

You can draw your own table if, say, you have a five- or six-week cycle rather than a four-week cycle.

Month	Week 1: period	Week 2	Week 3: ovulation	Week 4

Below is a guide to make your own emotions glossary, with examples of what your responses might be. You do not have to use boxes and if you don't like to use words you could draw pictures or use colours, but it may help you understand the difference between different emotions by thinking about the prompts in each box.

Emotion: Angry Means:	**Makes you behave...** Shouting. Slamming doors.
Makes you think...	**Makes you feel...** Hot inside my body and like I might explode!
Situations that can trigger it My parents telling me to do my homework (which is really hard).	**Things that make you feel better** Time out in my room listening to music.

3.6 What else happens during a menstrual cycle?

Changes in hormones (chemicals in the blood) can have other effects on the body during the menstrual cycle (not just when a person has a period). These effects are different for each person, but usually go away once the period starts.

Not everyone will have all these effects.

Spots (pimples)
Some people get spots on their face. These will go away and you can buy cleansers which help to get rid of them. See below the grid for more information on spots/pimples.

Bloating and retaining water
All bodies have water inside them. Bloating is when the body keeps water for long than usual, which can make you feel full and uncomfortable. This is normal during PMS or the first few days of your period. Drinking more water can help you to wee so you feel more comfortable.

Muscle aches
During PMS, some people get achy muscles. Painkillers, hot baths and heat packs can help.

Constipation and diarrhoea
Constipation: Some people find it harder to poo. Drinking plenty of water or taking a walk can help.

Diarrhoea: This is very runny poo. Eating fibre (e.g. breakfast cereals) can help. If your anus hurts, you can try putting a small amount of Vaseline on it.

Headaches
Headaches can be managed by drinking water, going for a walk or taking painkillers.

Food cravings
Some people crave salty or sugary foods during their periods. It can be easy to give in to these cravings, but try to not eat more salt or sugar then you usually would. Keeping a food diary can help you to manage this.

Spots (pimples)

The changes in the chemicals in a person's blood in their menstrual cycle can mean that the body makes more sebum (a liquid substance that comes out of the skin). A type of bacterium called *Propionibacterium acnes* (which is found naturally in our environment) uses the sebum as food. The red blotches are caused by your body trying to get rid of this bacterium.

Despite most people having an increase of sebum before their period, some people's skin looks healthier at that time.

The bacterium is not the kind which will do you any harm except for the spots. While they are annoying try to remember that spots are a normal part of growing up no matter which gender you are. They can sometimes reduce between periods. They are not caused by having dirty skin, but washing your skin once or twice a day will help to prevent them getting any worse. If your spots are bothering you, you can ask your doctor for help; they may be able to give you creams which will make them feel more comfortable.

3.7 How will I know when my periods will start?

To begin with periods may not be regular, but within two years of periods starting most people find their menstrual cycle has become more predictable (although most people miss a period once in a while). Your first period may be different to future periods, as they often change as you get older (the change can be in length, e.g. being a day shorter, and the pain can reduce for some people; some people can have no pain at all).

Lots of people only have spotting when their periods first start. Spotting is spots or dots of red or brown blood in your underwear (or menstrual product). Some people find blood in their underwear and other people find blood on the toilet paper they have used to wipe themselves after having a pee or poo. All of these things are very normal, and you can see in Part 2 Section F what they might look like. (Everyone is different so do not expect yours to look exactly the same as the photos.) Blood on the toilet paper when you have had a poo does not mean that your anus is bleeding (unless you have a separate problem); it is just that the blood has run down from your vagina and has ended up near your anus.

People don't have periods for ever. Most people's periods stop when they go through the menopause. The menopause is a series of things that happen in your body (like puberty). The menopause is when the ovaries are too old to work and usually happens between the ages of 45 and 60. (This might seem like a really long time away.)

Remember that other things seemed a big deal when you first learnt about them and are now easier (most of the time), so try not to worry – periods can be like that too. However, if you do have any problems or worries you can talk to your doctor or trusted adults; you could also talk to your friends who have periods.

Most people learn to notice different changes in their body which mean their period is due. They may also be able to tell by how they are finding it to manage life at different times in their menstrual cycle. Using a app such as Clue (see https://helloclue. com) can help you to note down your symptoms and see if there are any patterns.

Not starting your periods at the same time as your classmates is nothing to worry about. Some people start their periods age 8, others age 15, and others somewhere in-between. Having a period does not make you more or less grown up than people who start their periods at a different time to you. Just like growing taller, some people grow really tall when they are 11 and other people don't grow really tall ever (I am 152 cm/60″ so very short compared with most people my age).

3.8 Who can I talk with about periods?

As with the rest of the social world, there are unwritten rules about what people expect from other people's behaviour, so below are some common expectations about who it is OK to talk with about periods and where these conversations can take place. (Note that some cultures, countries and religions will have different expectations and it may be helpful to ask your parents or an adult you trust if they can help you add to this list to make it specific to where you live.)

- Most people would not want to talk about periods when there are a lot of people around, e.g. in a busy area of school. You can talk to your friends about it, but some people who do not have periods may feel embarrassed at first – check that they are comfortable to talk about it with you.
- You might prefer to talk to your friends about periods when you can't be heard by other people. So if you were in the playground and wanted to talk to your friend about periods it might be best to ask if you could have a quiet word (meaning that you want to talk about something which could be a bit embarrassing), and you and your friend can go somewhere out of earshot (which means somewhere other people will be unable to hear you).
- It is totally fine to ask a shop/sales assistant where the menstrual products are kept in the store/shop that they work in. Even if the shop assistant does not have periods, they will most likely have been asked this question many times before. If it helps you can close your eyes when you ask or look at the floor. You could also practise asking at home while looking at yourself in the mirror.
- When people first start their periods they can feel uncomfortable telling their parent. In my research, some people said they felt a bit less embarrassed at first if they didn't say the word 'period', but instead said something like 'Mum, I have blood in my underwear' (knowing that their mum would know this meant they had started their period). If you are in school or with a friend or trusted adult and find you do not have a tampon or pad and need to ask you could say, 'I have been caught short,' or if they still don't understand you could say, 'I have blood in my underwear – do you have anything I could use?' Most people will

understand this to mean that you need a tampon, pad, etc. Do not shout this as it may cause unwanted attention.

- It is very common to need to go to the toilet more often and to take more time than usual when you are on your period. This is because your bladder (which is the part of your body where your pee is stored until you pee it out) is close to your uterus and so if the uterus is contracting then this can push against the bladder. It is totally OK to ask a teacher to let you go to the toilet more often.

- It is always OK to speak to a doctor, nurse or other health professional about anything you are worried about. Usually these conversations are thought of as private, so if you have an appointment, wait until you have gone into the professional's room/cubicle before asking unless there is an emergency – in which case you can ask wherever you are.

- It's always OK to talk to adults you trust, but you may want to ask if you can go to one side with them (this means that you want to talk to them about something which is a bit private or which other people do not need to know about). Talking to a trusted adult in the car can sometimes be a good strategy if you are on your own with them, but if you need help right away then it's perfectly all right to ask them straight away wherever you are.

3.9 What is normal and what is not normal?

This section talks about the range of what is normal, so it's OK if your period is not exactly as described here.

What is normal?

Starting periods

Periods usually start between the ages of 8 and 16.

It is normal to get spotting (spots of blood in your underwear) before your periods start properly.

How often periods happen

People usually have a period every four to six weeks.

It may take up to two years for your periods to become regular.

The amount of blood

During their period most people lose 40–120 ml of blood. It can look like more because there is vaginal fluid and womb lining mixed in.

Some people bleed more in the morning and less in the evening and some people bleed a lot on the first day and not much on the last day.

How long the bleeding lasts

It is normal for bleeding to last between three and seven days.

What the blood looks like

The blood will start bright red. The clots (small lumps of blood and uterus lining) may look slightly darker, almost black, and at the end of your period the blood may look brownish. Just before your period (and sometimes during), you may see a clear or white discharge in your underwear. This is normal.

Pain

Many people have pain when they have a period (but not everyone has pain – if you are one of those people, then lucky you). If you have pain it can last anything from one to seven days, but the pain should go away with one or a combination of painkillers, heat pad and warm bath.

What is not normal?

If you have any of the symptoms listed below, you should seek medical advice.

Starting periods

It is unusual not to have started your periods by age 16.

Blood should not gush out of your vagina when you first start your periods.

How often periods happen and how long they last

It is not normal to have a period as often as every one to three weeks or as rarely as every seven weeks. If this does happen, it should not go on for longer than six months.

Bleeding should not last longer than seven days.

The amount of blood

It is not normal to lose more than 120 ml. It can be difficult to know exactly how much blood you have lost. Section 3.1 explains how to understand how much you are losing.

You should not have to change your pad or tampon as much as every one to two hours.

PMS/PMT (premenstrual syndrome/tension)

If you are finding that your symptoms mean you can't carry on your daily activities or if the effects of PMS/PMT are interfering too much with your life, then see a doctor.

What the blood looks like

You should not get yellow discharge, black blood, or just spotting and nothing else (once you have properly started your periods).

Pain

If you have tried several different pain-relieving methods and they have not worked for you, see your doctor.

Toxic shock syndrome

Toxic shock syndrome (TSS) is rare, but is life-threatening and the symptoms can get worse very quickly.

The symptoms of TSS can include:

- a high temperature: 39°C (102.2°F) or above
- flu-like symptoms
- feeling sick
- vomiting and/or diarrhoea
- a rash that looks like sunburn
- the whites of the eyes, and the lips and tongue may turn a bright red

- dizziness and/or fainting
- problems with breathing
- confusion
- feeling drowsy.

(www.nhs.uk/conditions/toxic-shock-syndrome)

3.10 My period plan — how I will deal with different situations

Before I have my first period, I will get ready by . . . .

. . . .

When my periods start the people I can talk to about them are . . . .

. . . .

I will try using . . . . .to collect my blood first.

If I am in pain I will . . . .

. . . .

If that doesn't work I will . . . .

. . . .

If I have PMS/PMT I will . . . .

. . . .

If I find I have run out of pads/tampons, etc. I will...

- At school . . . .

- At home . . . .

- At my friend's house . . . .

If I am away from home do I know how to dispose of my used menstrual products?

. . . .

. . . .

Part 2

Photos and Step-by-Step Guides

The female reproductive system

Most tampon and menstrual cup packets have instructions on the back with pictures. These work well for many people, but for those who find them confusing we've used a 3D model to demonstrate how to insert tampons and menstrual cups. The model is clear and shows a cross-section (as if the 3D model has been cut in half so you can see what's inside).

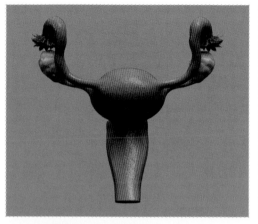

This is a 3D graphic of the womb, fallopian tubes, ovaries and vagina.

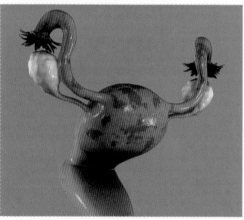

This is the diagram turned to the side.

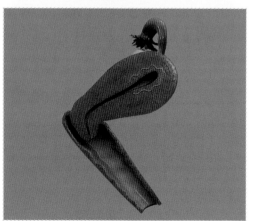

This is a cross-section, which we've used to demonstrate how to insert tampons and menstrual cups in Sections C and D.

A. How to use and change a disposable pad

How to use an individually wrapped disposable pad

Note: If the pad is not individually wrapped, there will be a piece of paper on the bottom which you can peel off, revealing a sticky area that you stick to your underwear.

1. Take the pad out of the packet. Put the packet down.

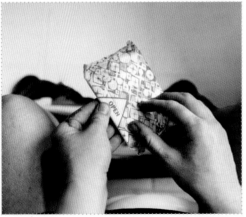

2. Pull the packet open (there is often the word 'open' on the packet or an arrow).

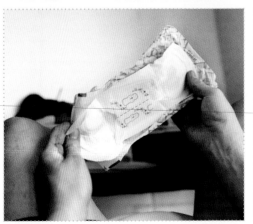

3. Fold open the packet.

4. Pull the pad off the packet and put the packet on your knee or on the floor. (If you put it on the floor make sure you put it in the bin when you are finished.)

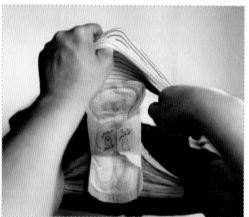

5. Stick the pad (the sticky bit goes onto your underwear) in your underwear. If your pad doesn't have wings, you've finished!

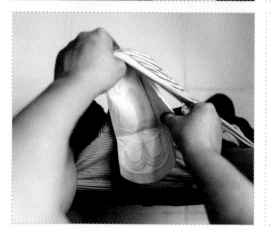

6. If the pad has wings, there is often a piece of paper over each wing or both wings: pull this off, then fold the wings around your underwear.

How to change a pad

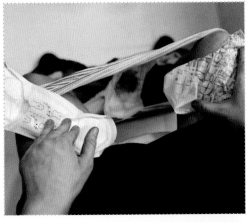

1. Take the new pad out of the packet (if it has one) and stick it on your knee, then put the open packet on your other knee.

2. Use your arm to hold down the pad or packet (whichever is easier), and while you do so peel the used pad off from your underwear.

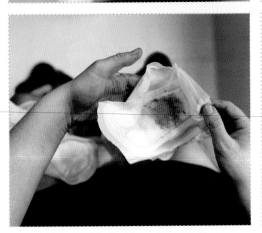

3. If the new pad does not have a packet, go to step 5. If it does, place the used pad on the packet. You can roll it into a sausage shape if you want to make the next step easier.

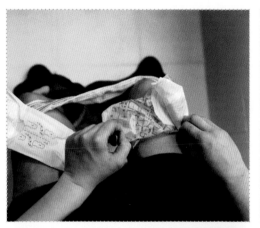

4. Roll the used pad up in the packet.

5. Pick up either a roll of toilet paper or a long strip of toilet paper and wrap the used pad and packet in toilet paper. Throw the used pad away.

6. Put the new pad onto your underwear.

B. How to use and change a cloth pad

The pad I have used in this demonstration is red: this is not blood and pads come in other colours.

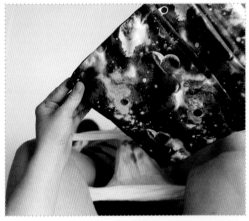

1. Take the cloth pad out of your wet bag.

2. Cloth pads usually have a pattern side and a soft side. Place the patterned side onto your underwear so you can see the soft side.

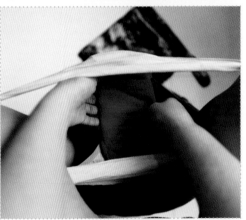

3. Join the poppers/snaps together around the bottom of your underwear.

4. When you need to change your pad, undo the poppers/snaps from the bottom of your underwear.

5. Take the pad off, roll it up and hold it on your knee or place it on the floor.

6. Place the pad in your wet bag.

When you get home put the used pads in the washing basket. At the end of your period, put them in the washing machine and wash them.

C. How to use a tampon

Inserting a tampon can take time to learn. Some people like to do it sitting on a toilet, others like to stand and put one foot on the toilet seat, and others prefer to do it in the shower (when they are having a shower anyway).

Inserting a tampon with an applicator

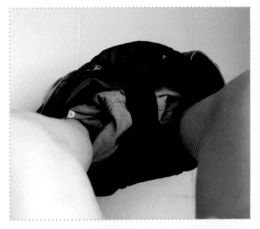

1. Sit on the toilet.

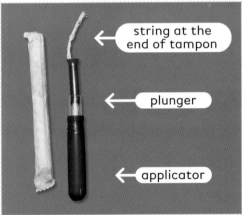

string at the end of tampon

plunger

applicator

2. Open the packet. Usually tampons are wrapped in paper or plastic, which you tear down the side.

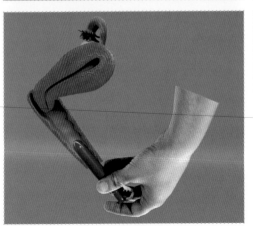

3. Hold the applicator with the plunger in your hand.

Unlike the picture, your vagina will have flaps of skin in front of it. Push them apart gently with the applicator.

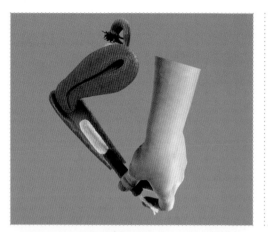

4. Tilt your hand upwards and slide the applicator inside your vagina.

Stop pushing when your fingers touch your skin.

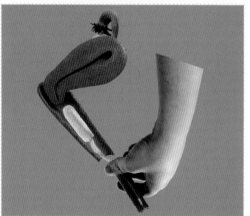

5. Push down the plunger.

This will push the tampon out of the applicator and into your vagina.

6. Throw the applicator away.

Your tampon is now in and you will see the string on the outside (but once you pull up your underwear you won't see the string).

Inserting a tampon without an applicator

Inserting a tampon takes practice – it probably won't go right the first time. If you do not want to use an applicator you will need to be OK about putting your fingers inside your vagina. Before starting to try to insert a tampon make sure you have washed your hands.

1. Sit on the toilet.

2. Open the packet.

Usually tampons are wrapped in plastic, which you unwrap, or paper, which you tear down the side.

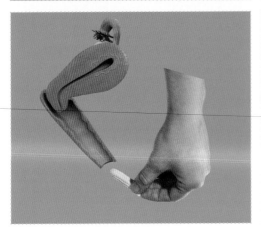

3. Hold the tampon between three fingers and insert it into your vagina.

Unlike the picture, your vagina will have flaps of skin in front of it. Push them apart gently with the tampon.

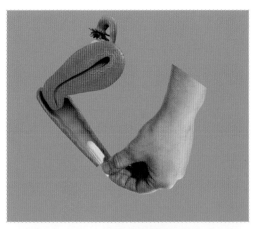

4. Tilt your hand upwards and slide the tampon in so that only the string is on the outside of your body.

You may find it easier to use your thumb to help guide it into position.

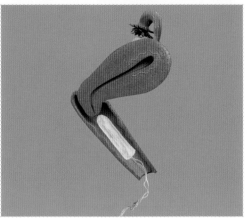

5. When you remove your hand the string will hang out of your vagina.

It's really important to know that it may take you several cycles to become confident at using tampons. At first, you can use period underwear, a pad or a panty liner as well as the tampon to avoid leaking.

If tampons don't work for you, or you don't want to wear them, it is totally OK not to use them – it is your body.

How to take out a tampon

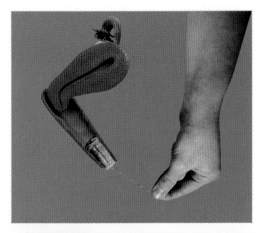

1. Pull the string gently – the tampon will have expanded with your blood and womb lining.

2. Wrap the tampon in toilet paper.

3. Put the used tampon in the bin.

D. How to use and empty a menstrual cup

Using a menstrual cup will take some practice. You need to be OK about touching your vagina. Make sure you wash your hands before you start following the instructions on this page.

How to insert a menstrual cup

1. Take your menstrual cup out of its bag (be sure to sterilise it before you use it for the first time – after sterilising you can leave it in its bag).

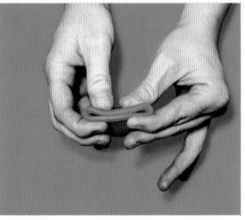

2. Fold your menstrual cup. There are lots of ways of folding it, but in these instructions I will show you the '7 fold'.

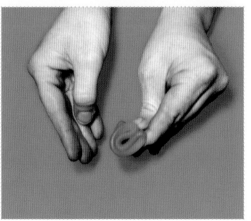

3. Take the cup and squeeze it to join the two edges. Fold half of the cup towards the bottom (so it looks like a 7).

4. Put some water-based lubricant (e.g. KY Jelly) on your finger, and then wipe it on the cup.

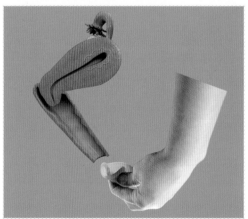

5. Slide the cup into your vagina by pushing open your labia with the same hand, and tilting your hand down and then upwards. Once you have the cup inside you let go of the cup and take your hand out of your vagina.

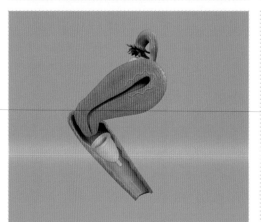

6. The cup should pop open.

Move your finger along the sides of the cup to check it is open.

This will take practice.

How to take out a menstrual cup

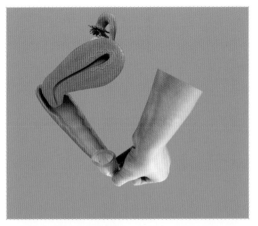

1. Hold onto the bottom of the cup – your cup may have grip rings here (bumpy lines at the bottom of the cup) – and pull the cup gently to break the suction.

You might find you have to pull harder than you think – if you are finding it difficult try squatting.

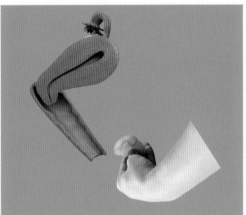

2. Slide your finger up the cup, press down in the middle, and pull the cup completely out.

3. Tip the cup's contents into the toilet.

Rinse the cup, either in a sink or by holding the cup over the toilet and pouring some water from a bottle over the cup.

Then reinsert the cup.

If you can't get to water, just wipe the cup with toilet paper and then reinsert.

E. What you might see on toilet paper/your underwear, and photos of your cervix

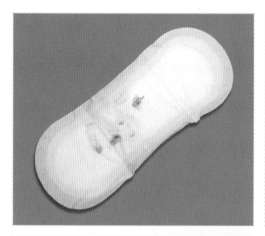

You may have heard of spotting – this is when only a little blood comes out.

When you wipe yourself after having a wee sometimes you will find the toilet paper has blood on it, because your period is starting.

When you wipe yourself after you have had a poo you may also find blood on the toilet paper. This does not usually mean that your anus is bleeding; it's just because your anus and vagina are close together so sometimes the blood runs from the vagina across to the anus.

'Flow' is a word that is used to describe how much blood a person is losing during a period. This is an example of a pad with what could be described as a heavy flow.

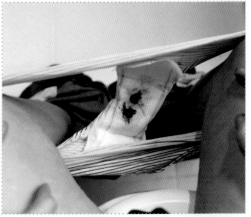

Sometimes blood and uterus lining will come out in a lump – this is called a blood clot. It is nothing to worry about, but sometimes it can feel strange when they come out of your vagina.

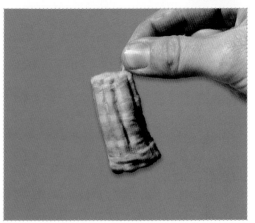

This is an example of a used tampon.

It can be hard to know exactly when your period will start. Sometimes you won't know that it has started until you go to the toilet and find blood in your underwear – this is totally normal.

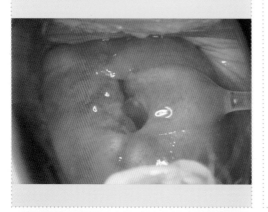

The cervix.

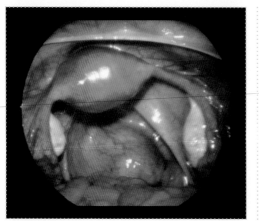

This picture was taken with a special camera, which was inserted just above the belly button.

Part 3

A Bit More Detail

What Happens in the Body During a Menstrual Cycle?

4.1 What happens biologically during a typical four-week menstrual cycle?

First, not everyone's cycle is four weeks (some people have a six-week cycle, for example). People have different symptoms and different extremes of those symptoms.

Below is a description of what happens inside the body during a four-week menstrual cycle. It is important to know that some people's cycles are longer or shorter than four weeks. Whatever the length of your cycle, the same stages happen in the same order, but the timings of these stages will be different.

Week 1

If you do not become pregnant (check with a trusted adult that you really understand what this means – but it is not the topic of this book so I won't go into detail here), then the level of progesterone released by the body will decrease. This triggers the uterus lining and blood vessels in the uterus lining to start to break down and come out of the vagina as a period. This breakdown of blood vessels can result in blood clots, as the body stops the bleeding by clotting (see Part 2 Section F for a photo of a blood clot from menstruation). This process is a natural function of the female body to clean out the uterus. (Please note that if periods stop due to illness or very low weight, this whole process stops and the uterus lining won't build up in the first place. There are also some conditions which mean a person does not have periods.)

Week 2

The uterus lining starts to build up. This lining is made from tissue, which is the scientific name given to a group of cells that are the same which together create a whole. (If you would like to see a photograph of the inside of a uterus turn to Part 2 Section F.) Luteinising hormone (LH) increases to help the body to start making oestrogen. Follicle-stimulating hormone (FSH) makes the follicles grow; these are the parts of the ovary which produce the egg.

Week 3

Luteinising hormone increases further and this causes an egg to be released from the ovary. There is a gap between the ovary and fallopian tubes. To get over the gap the fallopian tubes have flappy bits that look a bit like the sticks that people on the ground at airports wave to help guide a plane to land safely. (If the egg 'misses' it is reabsorbed by the body and the period still happens.) Progesterone is produced from inside the ovaries. This hormone makes the uterus lining able to sustain life. If pregnancy doesn't happen then the part inside the ovary producing progesterone (the corpus luteum) shrinks and is reabsorbed into the ovary.

Week 4

The lining of the uterus continues to thicken.

Hormones involved in the menstrual cycle

The menstrual cycle is regulated and controlled by hormones. Hormones are chemicals made by the body. They are tiny molecular structures and invisible to the human eye. A hormone is sometimes called a 'chemical messenger' because they travel in the bloodstream and deliver messages to cells.

There are four hormones involved in the menstrual cycle:

- **Oestrogen** (pronounced east row gen; in the USA it is spelled estrogen, but pronounced the same way) ensures the egg is properly matured (ready to be released).
- **Progesterone** (pronounced pro jest er own) makes the uterus lining able to sustain life.
- **Luteinising hormone (LH)** (pronounced loot in I zing) helps the body to start making oestrogen and release an egg.
- **Follicle-stimulating hormone (FSH)** makes the follicles grow – these are the parts of the ovary which produce the egg.

If you would like more detail about hormones, see www.autismfriendlyperiods.com/hormones.

4.2 What might happen emotionally during a typical four-week menstrual cycle?

Week 1

When someone is having a period it can make them feel tired. There are lots of reasons for this, but it may be caused by the muscle cramps which are being used to move the uterus lining and blood out of the uterus and through the vagina, as well as the amount of blood lost. This could cause changes in appetite or cravings for sweet things such as chocolate which release endorphins, the body's natural painkiller.

Week 2

In the week after a period people can be giggly and confident, and feel more attractive. Biologically, this could be designed to attract a mate. People can also be quite impulsive in this part of the cycle, sometimes have a heightened sense of smell, and are less sensitive to pain. They may have a stomach ache as the lining begins to form, and get headaches which could be due to the change in hormone levels.

Week 3

This is the part of the cycle where the egg is released. A period always starts 14 days after an egg is released. This is when PMS/PMT (premenstrual syndrome/tension) can start to happen as the hormone balance within the body begins to change, resulting in low mood, feeling sleepy, being withdrawn and struggling to think clearly. People may also crave comfort foods.

Week 4

PMS/PMT is at its most extreme within this week. This can make a person emotionally sensitive, feel more angry than usual, get annoyed or irritated more easily and feel sad and anxious. It can also make a person feel tired, have diarrhoea (runny poo) or not be able to poo easily (constipation). Some people find their breasts become tender and some retain water or experience bloating.

This sounds terrible!

On paper the description of what can happen during a menstrual cycle may sound awful; however, not everyone experiences all these symptoms and even those who do may not experience them to such a level that it stops them from getting on with everyday life. If you are finding that any of the issues described above do get in the way of your life you should talk to your doctor.

Premenstrual dysphoric disorder, or PMDD, is quite a new term, and research and knowledge about it is still developing. It is a severe form of PMS, and like PMS it is caused by the increase of hormones in the body after ovulation and before menstruation; however, the symptoms are more severe and can require a person to go to hospital: see www.autismfriendlyperiods.com/pmdd.

If you are concerned that you have PMDD then speak to your GP, but most people just have PMS/PMT.

4.3 What is my experience of menstruation?

When I started my periods I used to be in bed for three or four days, often feeling sick and with terrible stomach pain. My mum took me to the doctors who gave me a medicine called mefenamic acid. (You should always follow the advice of a doctor about medication as what is fine for one person may not work for another.) I took the medicine  at the first sign of a period and it reduced the blood flow to my pelvis, which meant the cramps were not so bad, and I could get on with my daily life easily.

I now take something called a progesterone only pill. This has made my periods stop and means I don't have PMS (which had made me prone to depression).

My family were very open about periods: as a toddler I would follow my mum everywhere, including to the toilet, and had seen her change sanitary towels so when I started my period it wasn't such a big deal.

By the age of 31, before taking the progesterone only pill, my periods were very different to the ones I had as a teenager. As I grew out of adolescence they became much easier to manage and my hormones followed a fairly regular schedule. This reduced the amount of pain I was experiencing.

I have used a cycle tracking app to keep a check on symptoms. For example, I was prone to getting migraines after I ovulated and before my period started and so I knew to avoid making any important plans for those days.

Autism-Specific Issues with Periods

There are a few areas of life relating to the menstrual cycle in which autistic people may experience things differently to non-autistic people. The aim of this chapter is to explain these issues and provide some resources to help you or the person you care for or support to overcome these issues. Due to the size of this book, it is impossible for me to cover every single scenario; however, I hope the information contained here will help you identify areas of difficulty and give you a starting point for thinking about how to deal with them.

Everyone has strengths and weaknesses, whether autistic or non-autistic. The challenges described here are specific to autism. However, I want to acknowledge that sometimes 'weaknesses' make us think differently about our strengths, which ultimately can help us become successful in ways that non-autistic people may not find so available.

5.1 Sensory issues

When I began researching this book, many autistic people said they felt that the main differences in their experience of menstruating compared with non-autistic people's experiences were the result of sensory issues. Sensory issues broadly fitted into two categories:

1. managing everyday life (i.e. experiences/situations you would be in regardless of your period)
2. period specific (e.g. using menstruation products, coping with the blood, or cramps).

In this book I have focused primarily on the period-specific issues, as there are quite a number of resources available on sensory issues in general. For more information on sensory issues you might like to read, for example, Olga Bogdashina's book *Sensory Perceptual Issues in Autism and Asperger Syndrome* (also published by Jessica Kingsley Publishers).

Different menstrual products (sometimes called sanitary or feminine hygiene products) can cause different sensory issues. It's really important to know you do not have to try using or keep using any one product and that there are many options.

I have spent quite a bit of time researching different alternatives to the standard tampons and sanitary towels. These are the three main options people identified in my survey as being sensory friendly:

1. period underwear and swimsuits – underwear which is designed to catch and hold menstrual blood and fluids
2. cloth/fabric pads, which are put into underwear to catch menstrual fluids
3. menstrual cups, which are made from silicone or TPE and are inserted inside the vagina to catch menstrual blood and fluids.

Below, I look at the different alternatives and the sensory issues that some people find with them.

Tampons

A lot of companies that make tampons have starter packs. The starter packs contain a few different kinds of tampons that they make so you can try different ones out.

Many non-autistic and autistic people struggle to use tampons at first. If you are finding it difficult check with your doctor that you don't have any conditions which could affect this.

Period underwear and swimsuits

Several manufacturers now create period underwear. This underwear is not like wearing a nappy. It can be worn all the time, and can be very comfortable and effective. There are also swimsuits available.

Period underwear works by using several layers of fabric; the layer that goes next to the skin is a wicking fabric which pulls the blood to the layers below it. Manufacturers advocate a snug fit to reduce the possibility of leaks.

Different manufacturers make different types of underwear with different levels of absorbency, suitable for different types of flow. Some are more like panty liners and therefore could be worn just before a period or on a light day, while others are for heavy days, and others have changeable cloth pads. See www.autismfriendlyperiods.com/periodunderwear for a list of manufacturers.

Menstrual cloth pads

There are many different manufacturers, small businesses and individuals who make and sell menstrual cloth pads. These work like disposable pads, using several layers of fabric to wick the blood from the skin and store it in an absorbent layer. Menstrual cloth pads are washable and therefore reusable and there is a huge number of combinations of fabrics available. Because they are washable, if you wash them with your clothing or bedding they will smell like them, and some people may find this beneficial. You can also use a fabric conditioner which may help.

Features of menstrual cloth pads:

- **Poppers/snaps:** These fasten the pad to underwear. Some pads have single snaps (one on each side of the pad) and some have double (two snaps on each side). The advantage of double is that on a heavy flow day, if you are concerned about leaking, you can make the pad fit tighter around your underwear. The disadvantage is that it can make the fabric hump slightly at the bottom and some people may find this uncomfortable.

- **Shape and length:** You can get various shapes and lengths, particularly longer and shorter ones, but some also have wings (the side bits that wrap around the underwear) of different shapes.
- **Ice and heat packs:** Some pads, designed for people who have just had a baby, even have a gap to slide in ice packs. You could also slide in heat packs or perhaps a piece of cloth with a scent you like, which can be refreshed.
- **Stiches:** Some cloth pad makers sew their stitches on the inside, not against skin. This can be more comfortable for people who are sensitive to things against their skin.
- **Top:** The part of the pad that touches the skin.
- **Core:** The middle part that holds the blood.
- **Backing:** This part touches the underwear.

Fabrics
Visit www.autismfriendlyperiods.com/menstrualcloths for a list of common fabrics used to make cloth pads. If making your own (see www.autismfriendlyperiods.com/makeclothpads for instructions) you can use any combination.

Menstrual cups

Menstrual cups are usually made from silicone. There are different types, or grades, of silicone. Menstrual cups are usually made from medical grade silicone, which is silicone that has been approved for use in medical devices. Some manufacturers also make menstrual cups from TPE (thermoplastic elastomer), which is a type of plastic used for making baby bottle teats. It is softer so may be better for someone just starting to use a cup.

There is also the Keeper menstrual cup, which is made by the people who make the Moon Cup and is made from latex. Visit www.autismfriendlyperiods.com/cups for a summary of some commonly available menstrual cups.

Some cups have grip rings which can make them easier to remove, although some people find these uncomfortable.

Advice on starting with menstrual cups

If you are keen to try using a menstrual cup, but think that the sensory issues or adjusting to something new might be difficult, then here are some tips.

- When you first start trying to use a menstrual cup, try it on a day of your period when your flow is not too heavy.
- To begin with you do not have to wear it all day; you can just put it in for five minutes and then take it out again.
- Some menstrual cups are firmer or softer than others, and this is often detailed on the manufacturers' websites – try a softer one to start with.
- Try inserting your finger inside your vagina before trying a menstrual cup (find your cervix, which will feel like a hard pebble or marble).
- Have a bath before trying to insert a menstrual cup, as warm water can help to relax your muscles; you can also try putting it on in the shower.
- You may find it helpful to put a heat pad, hot water bottle or wheat bag warmed up in the microwave on your stomach for a while before or after inserting a cup, to help the muscles relax.
- Use a water-based lubricant (e.g. KY Jelly), which will make the cup slippery and easier to insert.
- Try different folds (in Part 2 Section D for an example of a '7 fold').
- Don't rush when putting in your menstrual cup or taking it out; it's OK to take your time. If you are are struggling to get the cup out, try squatting in the bath or shower – this will reduce the length of your vagina – and try to pull it out gently. Be sure to clean the bath or shower afterwards.
- You should not feel the cup but you might feel your muscles stretch (as it uses muscles you may not have used much before).

- Some people find the cups more comfortable if they cut the stem shorter, or even cut it off altogether and trim it to make the base of the cup very smooth. Before doing this, make sure that you are comfortable removing the cup without using the stem.
- It may feel a bit strange at first but that's OK.
- Once the cup is in, try doing something engrossing.
- Wear a panty liner or pad in your underwear until you feel comfortable that the cup won't leak.
- If it leaks the first few times you use it, don't worry. It takes practice to get the cup to open fully and in the right position (directly under your cervix).
- It takes practice – it may take several cycles to feel confident.
- You can just use a menstrual cup at home to begin with before going out with it.
- If you find that you experience pain in your urethra when you remove a menstrual cup, try putting your finger up into the side of the cup and folding it before removing it.

Sensory issues that non-autistic people may find confusing

While some autistic people are hypersensitive to sensory input (they take too much information in from one or some of their senses), others are hyposensitive (they do not take in enough information). This might mean they are sensory seekers, i.e. they seek out stimulation. Here is an example of what that behaviour could look like:

> Smells are something I'm sensation-seeking in, because I'm under-sensitive to them. So someone had to teach me that I should be changing my pads more often because by the time they were in the trash they smelled very bad. But still I always smell them now, when I'm switching them – it's an interesting smell. I think neurotypical people would believe that is gross. (Jenny)

The effects of sensory issues are not just limited to menstrual products but also to how a person lives their life, for example:

The range of foods I can tolerate (mainly due to texture and temperature) seems to narrow during my PMS. I just try to factor that into my meal plan. (Jo)

5.2 Executive functioning

Executive functioning is the skills a person uses to figure out:

- what they have to do either now or in the future
- when they have to do it
- what order they have to do it in.

People who have trouble with executive functioning in school are often the children who bring every book with them for each subject regardless of whether they are doing that subject that day. They are the kids who lose things constantly, and struggle to work out how to get their homework done and in what order.

Having a period can affect someone's executive functioning. It can make them struggle with things like hygiene, choosing clothes to wear, getting a task done in a timely manner, and finding time to wash.

Problems with executive functioning are not the same as being lazy. A person with difficulties in executive functioning can be helped to plan what they need to do and have systems in their life that can help them do these things, working with their level of executive functioning.

Thank you page

Thank you to everyone who supported me in the research for this book, especially the people who filled out my surveys and my team at CRAE. Thank you to the pupils and teachers at Limpsfield Grange School. Thank you to my colleagues at the Society for Menstrual Cycle Research.

Thank you to Lisa, Vicki and Adam at JKP.

Thanks to Mish, my agent.

Notes